X-RATED
Prayers

X-RATED
Prayers

Theresa Billingsley

Copyright Information:

X-Rated Prayers By:
THERESA BILLINGSLEY
Xratedprayers@gmail.com

©2019 Copyright and owned by:
THERESA BILLINGSLEY
Published by: Theresa Billingsley
in conjunction with Good News Ministries
ISBN-13: 978-1-888081-32-9
ISBN-10: 1-888081-32-5

Used by permission. All rights reserved. Printed in the United States of America. All rights reserved under International Copyright Law. Contents and/or cover may not be reproduced in whole or in part in any form without the express written consent of the Publisher.
All scriptures are taken from the NKJ or NLT version of the Bible, as noted.

No part of this book may be reproduced or transmitted in any form or by any means, electronic or mechanical, including photocopying, recording, or by an information storage and retrieval system, without permission in writing from the Author.

Format by: Lisa Buck Cover
Art by: Lisa Buck

Visual Media and Consulting: Reginald Charlestin
Edited by: Janique Burke

Dedication

To every person that reads, recommends, and uses this book as a guide to help themselves and others address certain issues of life, I dedicate this assignment to you with love and a zero tolerance for the enemy of our souls.

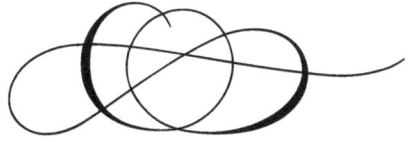

Contents

Dedication	i
Preface	v
Acknowledgements	ix
When Helping Them is Killing Me!	1
It's an Inside Job	7
Self-sabotage/Mental Torment	
In Love with Lust	13
Don't Abuse Your Authority	
Touched in All the Right Places	17
That Moment You're Vulnerable & Get Manipulated Emotionally & Physically	
A Hard Head Makes a Soft Azz	21
The Moment Someone is a Bad Influence	
Drug Addicts, Drug Dealers, & Gang Members Have Souls Too!	27
Don't Give Up On Them!	
The Spell is Broken	33
Tug of War	37
Freedom from Masturbation or Perversion	41
Stop! You're Under Arrest!	49

Your Breath Stinks	53
To Whom Have You Given Authority to Use Your Breath?	
I Thought I Got Away with Murder! Spiritual Homicide/Suicide	63
"In the Church"	69
I'm Awake but I Can't Get Up	77
Demons or Sleep Paralysis	
General Declarations to Say Daily	80
I've Fallen and I Want to Get Up!	83
God, it's All Your Fault	87
Sleeping With the Enemy	91
Pillow Talk	97
Tears Are Liquid Prayers	
Stop Lying on God	103
Using Your Position of Authority to Control/Manipulate Others	
Pick on Someone Your Own Size	111
I Will Not Be Bullied	
Neither Will I Commit Suicide	
Epilogue	121
Prayer of Salvation	123
About the Author	129

Preface

I was resting when I heard the words, "X-Rated Prayers." I wrote it down, and four months later I started writing. I thought to myself, "There are situations that some may think are off limits to pray about."

Sometimes we feel like we can't be transparent with God, our Heavenly Father. There are other times we feel we can't come to Him with certain issues. I wrote this in hopes that it will dispel the myths and open the lines of communication between you and your Creator. You don't need to have a theological dissertation to pray. Sometimes all you have to say is, "Jesus/Yeshua, help me!"

If you don't go to church, this book is still for you. In times of trouble and distress, run to God not away from Him. Don't let the devil trick you into believing you can't go to God because you're worried that He thinks you only go to Him when you're in trouble.

He is NOT like man, and yes you should have a constant relationship and fellowship with HIM. But until you get to that point, don't beat yourself up. When you are praying for yourself, as well as others, focus your prayers on the root cause of the problem, not just the symptoms you see.

Look at behaviors you might be displaying, as well as the behaviors others might experience and target them through prayer. Like the need for air for our human body to survive, prayer is the oxygen for our spirit. Praying God's Word will release angels on assignment for you.

Prayer communicates to God that you trust Him and want His help. Through prayer, you give God permission to help you.

This book is a prayer template. Keep in mind that it is not limited to the verbiage I have used. Whatever you feel led to pray, make your requests known to God. Pour out your heart before Him. Don't hold back! If you don't know what to say or are unsure, these prayers will help break the ice and build your confidence.

There are many experiences I have personally encountered. There have been times I have observed other people's experiences as well. These prayers are based on a few of those encounters. Prayer alone won't help. It's not a get-out-of-jail (or hell) -free card. God is NOT our butler.

You must do your part. Obey God's Word. Be disciplined. Make better choices. Avoid traps. Be accountable to someone stronger and more disciplined than yourself. Someone who won't agree with your mess. Stop believing the lies of the evil one. Also, there may come a time when you need to seek counseling, don't be too prideful or embarrassed to go.

We are on various levels, both in our willingness to obey God and in our understanding as it pertains to dealing with things HIS way. Often, it's a result of how we are taught, or the lack thereof. For those who don't need prayers on the topics in this book, please don't frown upon those that do. Those that need these prayers should not be embarrassed. Be free!

I apologize in advance if this writing is not what many may call "theologically sound" or "grammatically correct". God understands the way we talk, even when it's not eloquent, therefore, I wrote certain prayers in the manner I speak.

Some may read this book who are not saved, yet they struggle with the issues these prayers address. It's my hope that they will be made free and learn about the Savior who set them free. Some won't come to the church at first, but we are not bound by religious protocol, and neither is God.

Disclaimer: When I use the word God, I am referring to Yahweh/YHWH our Heavenly Father - the God of Abraham, Isaac, and Jacob.

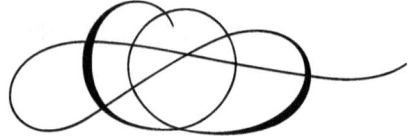

Acknowledgements

The Most High God – Yahweh, my Lord and Savior, Yeshua - Jesus Christ, and the Holy Spirit:

Thank You for being with me during those times I went through periods of disobedience and walked into traps the enemy set to destroy me. You provided everything I needed to overcome every situation so that I may help others.

This assignment pulled me way out of my comfort zone. You got a three-for-one from this assignment. I hope you are pleased. I Love, Love, Love you, Father!

Mom

My SUPER Woman! Thank you for being such a dynamic woman, mother, best friend, protector, prayer-partner, and provider. God couldn't have selected a better mother. You made raising us look so easy. I love you!

Dad

My Hero! I admire your strength. You have overcome many obstacles in life. Watching you has taught me about God's grace, mercy, and how to have the courage to bounce back. I am so proud of you. I love you!

My Brother

My Bodyguard! Our talks give me life. I love how you think. I look up to you literally - because of your height (you are still my little brother though, LOL!) and I look up to you figuratively - because you are Amazing in every way. I love you!

My Three Sons!

My Prayer partners! I can't express what gifts you are to me and the lessons of love that I have learned from being your Mother. You bring me so much joy. You all have caused me to grow, pray and seek God in ways I didn't know were possible. I love you!

Bishop Charles W. Harris, Jr.

My second Dad! Thank you for letting God use you. I knew God wanted me to write, but I had no idea what to write about. This is so far out of my element. I was at home praying - asking God what I should write about. You had no idea about that prayer when I came to you. You told me to sit down and pick a topic. I thought you were going to have me preach that night. LOL! I wrote it, although yet to be published, here is another book on the same topic. I love you!

Apostle Tawana Thompson

Thank you for sharing your testimony of writing your book in 30 days and for walking me through the process of doing my own. You inspired me. You are so selfless and loving. I truly appreciate you.

Minister Reginald Charlestin

Thank you for helping me with this assignment. From the book cover to uploading and downloading information. You did an amazing job. I felt so insecure and terrified, yet you patiently encouraged me. I appreciate you beyond measure.

Brother Hahz

You are an Anointed Lyricist and Minister of the Gospel of Jesus Christ/Yeshua. The "Die Empty" track on your newest CD "THE HAHZPITAL" (Hospital) helped push me out of fear and self-doubt. I appreciate your ministry. I hope many (young and old) contact you to purchase your music. If interested, please contact: brotherhahzlive@gmail.com.

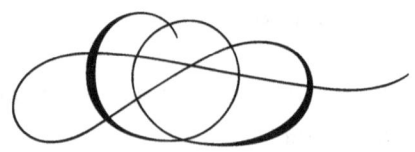

When Helping Them is Killing Me!

> *Heavenly Father, I thank you for the privilege of coming boldly before Your throne to obtain Mercy and Grace in this time of need. You are King of kings, Lord of lords and a good, good Father!*

I always try to be compassionate to others, but sometimes people take that compassion and use it to reel me in and suck me dry emotionally and financially. It drains me mentally and affects me physically. I get headaches, chest pains, anxiety, and feel depressed when I leave their presence. It's like a garbage truck dumped their junk on me. Now they feel better, but I feel terrible, as if I need to take a mental health day.

Prayer

God, give me Your wisdom, clarity, and the words to say so I may stand up for myself without sounding condescending. When I try to let them know they are out-of-bounds, they manipulate emotionally and play the victim as if I am wrong for wanting to stand my ground.

Trying to please them so they don't feel like I'm tired of them is negatively impacting my household, well-being, etc.

I'm concerned about their feelings, yet it seems they care nothing about mine as long as they are getting what they want. They threaten suicide and act so helpless.

Release your warring Angels God, to cut every demonic connection between us that causes manipulation, which is a form of witchcraft. Sever everything in me that's a magnet to attract negative situations and impulses. Set me free from guilt, regret, shame, false compassion, and the need to be needed.

I am not everyone's savior. Forgive me for being an enabler. I free myself. I remove myself from the throne of their life, from the place You should have in their life, God. I tap out, I give up, and I bow out gracefully.

God, let them yield to You and allow You to take Your place on the throne of their heart. At times I should have said no, but I said yes because I didn't want my image of being their savior to be tainted (pride). Because of this, they played on my need to be needed.

I inadvertently blocked them from an opportunity to seek Your face and learn how to trust You on a new level.

Lord, let me hear beyond what is said to me, see beyond what is shown to me, and grant me the grace to love without limits – all without fear of being manipulated, because perfect love casts out all fear.

God, You are the King of Glory. You are the Master of the universe, yet You don't intrude in our lives.

You gave us free will to choose You and Your way or we can reject You and do things our way. I choose You. I trust You. I need You. You desire the best for me. Let those who are draining me and those that I'm allowing to suffocate me trust You for themselves.

In the name of Jesus/Yeshua I pray, Amen.

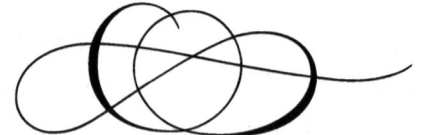

It's an Inside Job
Self-sabotage/Mental Torment

> *Heavenly Father, I thank you for the privilege of coming boldly before Your throne to obtain Mercy and Grace in this time of need. You are King of kings, Lord of lords and a good, good Father!*

~ Prayer ~

I come to You asking for forgiveness because I've used my words to agree and partner with the negative circumstances in my life.

Father forgive me for agreeing with the negative words that I or others have spoken in fear, jealousy, bitterness, or unbelief against me. I was wrong, I'm sorry.

In the name of Jesus/Yeshua, I no longer partner with, nor agree with negative thoughts, words, actions, motives, and intents that come to derail me. They are inoperative and ineffective in my life.

I speak that I shall _____ (find a scripture from the Holy Bible to counteract and attack those negative characteristics and release life, peace, and righteousness to you or the person you are praying for based on the scenario, whether it's regarding health, finance, or the ability to accomplish something.)

For example, you can fill in the blank with:

"Beloved, I wish above all things that thou mayest prosper and be in health, even as thy soul prospers."
(3 John 1:2 KJV)

~ Continue to Pray ~

I come to You in the name of Jesus/Yeshua. I don't know what I don't know, and now that I look back over my life, I'm realizing I am a product of my upbringing, choices, surroundings, and of my words and thoughts of myself.

I didn't realize that words spoken to me as a child empowered or crippled me. Years went by and I suppressed words, thoughts and actions that are subliminally in my subconscious mind.

These thoughts caged me in and restricted me like a python snake. It's an inside job, an internal verbal assault.

The words and thoughts in my head have caused me to be stagnant and fearful. Wash me with the water of Your word. I renounce the powers of darkness, and I no longer partner with the mental manipulation operating against me.

In the name of Jesus/Yeshua I pray, Amen.

Note: If this applies to you or someone you know, take time and reflect on the words from parents, teachers, spouses, or anyone in authority that may have spoken negativity into you. This would include judges, lawyers, preachers, etc. Ask God to remove the negative impact their words had on your subconscious.

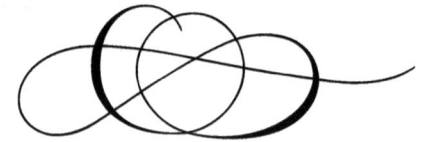

In Love with Lust

Don't Abuse Your Authority

> *Heavenly Father, I thank you for the privilege of coming boldly before Your throne to obtain Mercy & Grace in this time of need. You are King of kings, Lord of lords and a good, good Father!*

I confess that I'm guilty of selfishness, idolatry, and many other things that are bosom-buddies with those behaviors. I come before You, desperate and in great need of Your help. I have been doing this for so many years and getting away with it. With my popularity and my lies, I became prouder and more arrogant. The lust of my flesh is unbridled and out of control.

I'm impure. I am lustful and out of control. It started as far back as I can remember, when _____ (name what opened the door for devils to come in with lust, etc. Was it sex out of wedlock? Was it a curse or spell put on you? Was it because you participated in a threesome or another sexual act? Was it due to watching porn?)

I can't go on like this. I use men/women to fulfill my fantasies and needs. I continually lie to all of them to get what I want. I confess, it's sin. It's not pleasing to You, God, and I'm guilty as charged by Your Word. It's not what You created me for.

God, please help me. Take away this unbridled lust. I give You permission to purge me. I know I can't get free from what I desire to keep because that makes me a willing captive. I want to be free!

Cleanse me from all of this unrighteous behavior and help me cut the ties. Heal me at the source of this behavior. Uproot the seed and all its roots. Lay Your ax to the root of my heart and mind.

Lord, I desire to think and act differently. Send people into my life who will be bold enough to confront me and hold me accountable; who aren't intimidated by me, nor my position of authority.

I have been abusing and misrepresenting the authority You have entrusted me with. God, I give You my mind to cleanse and renew. I give You my will, and I ask for Your will for my life. I give You my heart, to heal it and remove all demonic clutter and defilement. Give me the desire to be obedient to You in thought, word, and actions. Let the words of my mouth and the meditation of my heart be acceptable in Your sight. Be my strength and redeemer.

I know it takes more than prayer. It takes actions, discipline, self-control, and saying no to seduction, sinful relationships and invitations that I know will end in sin. I need psychological help and permanent people to be accountable to. I failed to exercise discipline and self-control. I sometimes act like a dog in heat with my fleshly appetite.

I make a conscious decision to stop making excuses for my ungodly behavior. I will no longer believe in or partner with the lies of my past, nor the current lies I believe that numb my conscious and cause me to blatantly sin against You, Lord, and against my own body and consciousness. Cleanse me from the filthiness of my heart, mind, and soul.

In the name of Jesus/Yeshua I pray, Amen.

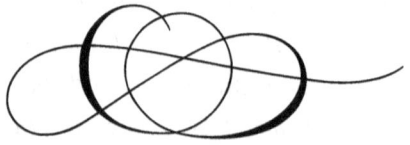

Touched in All the Right Places

That Moment You're Vulnerable & Get Manipulated Emotionally & Physically

> *Heavenly Father, I thank you for the privilege of coming boldly before Your throne to obtain Mercy & Grace in this time of need. You are King of kings, Lord of lords and a good, good Father!*

Prayer

I come to You broken and feeling like a fool. It feels like I got blindsided. I was lied to and deceived. I was naïve and gullible.

I was led to believe we were going to be together. We discussed marriage, and they did and said all the things long-term couples say and do.

I was so blinded by all the attention and affection that I ignored any warning signals or sirens that You sent to caution me. I even overrode my conscious. I allowed myself to be deceived, hoping the warning signs weren't real.

Please, God, make the hurt stop. I can't stop crying. If I'm not crying, I'm angry and short-tempered with others. I want to find a way to release my anger.

I don't know what to do. Do I tell others? I'm embarrassed, and I shouldn't have been doing this, so I don't want to expose myself or make the other person look bad. Yet, I don't want others to experience the same deception.

I should have known something wasn't right when he kept me a secret, always wanted to go to a hotel, and I couldn't ever go to his house.

We were always having quickies in the car. Cleanse my body, God, from their touch. My body feels their touch when I think of the times we had together.

Cleanse my mind from the conversations we had and remove the longing and craving I have for them. I feel so addicted to them. I feel like I was under a spell. God, I need you to heal my spirit, soul, and body.

In the name of Jesus/Yeshua I pray, Amen.

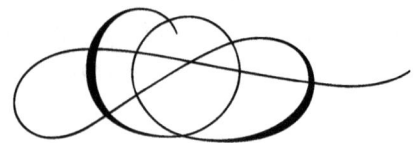

A Hard Head Makes a Soft Azz

The Moment Someone is a Bad Influence

> *Heavenly Father, I thank you for the privilege of coming boldly before Your throne to obtain Mercy & Grace in this time of need. You are King of kings, Lord of lords and a good, good Father!*

Prayer

I come before You, thanking You for helping _____ (name who you are praying for) in times of trouble. You are our protector, shield, and buckler. You have the power to rescue _____ (name the person you are praying for) from every trap and snare of the devil. You've already made an open show of the enemies defeat when You raised Jesus/Yeshua from the grave.

I know nothing surprises You or catches You off-guard. Sometimes things can catch us off-guard if we don't take heed to Your warnings. I need your help, _____ (name who you are praying for) disobeys You, then tries to handle everything on (his/her) own instead of coming to You as (his/her) Heavenly Father.

He/She thinks because he/she is grown, he/she can and must handle everything on their own. He/She does not know how to be child-like before You.

God, _____ (name who you're praying for) need(s) Your help. (Throughout the prayer, change the verbiage to add details concerning your situation.)

He/She won't listen to reason. They are under a spell, seduced by lust, eating from the devil's table of temptation because it's a beautiful layout of all that they desire. They fool/deceive themselves into thinking that You are okay with their lusts being fulfilled, because they are okay with it. They go contrary to Your Word that says to DENY ourselves and take up our cross and follow YOU.

Let there be light in every part of their heart and soul, so they can see and perceive the truth about _____. (name the person, place or thing that is a distraction or derailment.) Show them who is who and release Your Angels to protect them from any demonic or self-sabotaging ramifications.

Let Your angels run interference between _____ (name who you are praying for) and _____ (name who or what is the negative influence) so they no longer desire their relationship, nor the sin of the relationship. Sever the union, break the agreement, cut the partnership.

A Hard Head Makes a Soft Azz

In the name of Jesus/Yeshua, I forbid and remove all demonic influence, relationships, and the covenants made by words, written contracts, oaths, and blood agreements (cutting themselves and physically mixing their blood). Release Your fire, God, to burn up all ungodly activity and influences.

Every person, place, and thing the devil is using to draw _____ (name the person you are praying for) away from _____ (name the person/situation) and away from You, God, please remove them now and forever. Remit their sins, Lord.

Let the spirit of truth, humility, and boldness to obey God be manifested.

They will have no fear in leaving the devil's den, nor fear any backlash. Let Your warring Angels destroy any hindering spirit of bondage, captivity, and sabotage.

X-Rated Prayers

Forgive them, Lord, for being willing captives and for being drawn to the dark side, which leads to death. Take the blinders off the eyes of their heart and mind. Let them no longer seek gratification in things that bring death and destruction.

God/Yahweh, I ask that You forgive all their iniquities, heal all their diseases, and redeem their life from destruction.

Crown them with loving kindness and tender mercies. Satisfy their mouths with good things so that their youth is renewed like the eagles, and Lord, execute righteousness and judgment to all that are oppressed according to (Psalms 103:3-6 KJV).

I renounce every mind-blinding spirit and ask God/Yahweh that You release the LIGHT of Jesus/Yeshua to _____ (name the person) and manifest a sober mind. _____ (name the person) will be free to live for and obey You, God/Yahweh, all the days of their life and they will fulfill their destiny and they will NOT miss Heaven.

A Hard Head Makes a Soft Azz

I break the power of any curses put on them from words spoken over them, beginning in the womb, in the name of Jesus/Yeshua.

Any bloodline/generational curses sent to _____ (name the person) thru our/their DNA, we ask that You cleanse their blood now with the blood of Jesus/Yeshua.

Let them divorce this world, its cares and lusts, and cling to the righteousness of God/Yahweh. Let them no longer desire the devil and his deception and seductions. Let them see from the eyes of God/Yahweh.

In the name of Jesus/Yeshua I pray, Amen.

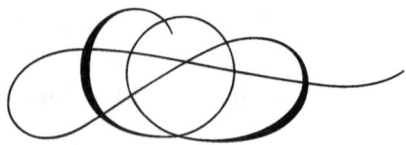

Drug Addicts, Drug Dealers, & Gang Members Have Souls Too!

Don't Give Up On Them!

> *Heavenly Father, I thank you for the privilege of coming boldly before Your throne to obtain Mercy & Grace in this time of need. You are King of kings, Lord of lords and a good, good Father!*

Drug Addicts & Gang Members Have Souls Too!

Many of us have someone in our family, or know someone with family members, who are involved in drug use, abuse or sales. Those drugs can be illegal, prescribed or over-the-counter.

Lawlessness, identity crisis, bastard wounds, and death spirits spoken over people (due to fear) have caused catastrophes in many people's lives, because it released and empowered the enemy of our soul through negative words.

They have given up on themselves. Don't let the devil get a two for one.

They have given up AND YOU GIVE UP ON THEM TOO, thereby allowing the devil to have his way with them, NOOOOOOOOOOOOOOO!!!

YOUR PRAYERS MATTER!

Prayers have NO EXPIRATION DATE!!!! Even if you don't live to see the day of their deliverance, your prayers make a difference. No one can outrun prayer. Your prayers and love are more effective than your embarrassment or disdain towards them.

No matter what, don't speak in alignment with the evil they are doing or saying. Keep saying _____ (name the person) will fulfill their God/Yahweh given destiny. They will be a mighty child of God/Yahweh, they will NOT miss Heaven, and they will receive Jesus/Yeshua as their Lord and Savior.

Prayer

Remove all blinders from the eyes, heart and mind of _____ (name who you are praying for).

Give them a vision of who they are called to be in you, show them a glimpse of their destiny. Show them how to use their gifts and talents for You, God, and not the devil. Remove helpless and hopeless spirits from them. Help them stop believing and agreeing with the lies of the devil.

Restore their dignity and show them their identity in YOU God/Yahweh according to Psalms 139:16. _____ (name the person) will accept Jesus/Yeshua as their Lord and Savior. They will fulfill their destiny God has ordained for their life. They will not miss Heaven.

Drug Addicts & Gang Members Have Souls Too!

They feel trapped like in a spider's web, as if to say, this is all they know. They are afraid to fight for FREEDOM from _____ (gang violence, drug sales, and improper use of prescription or illegal drugs) and are too mentally lazy to do the work necessary to succeed. Give them courage and boldness from Your Spirit Lord. They are in a stupor under a demonic spell and fog. Help them snap out of it by your Power Lord.

Give them the mental and physical fortitude to make a conscious decision to transition from the kingdom of darkness into the Kingdom of Light. Let there be light in every fiber of their being. King of Glory release your Angels to destroy the stronghold of the Zombie (dead-man-walking spirit) off of _____ (name who you are praying for).

X-Rated Prayers

In the name of Jesus/Yeshua, I remit the sins of _____ (name the person) have mercy on them Lord.

I renounce the spirit of death that has entered _____ (name the person), and we speak Abundant life and health to all their flesh. (Proverbs 4:22) We say they shall live and not die to declare the works of the Lord (Psalms 118:17) with long life you will satisfy them and show them their salvation plan for their life. (Psalms 91:16) Pray all of Psalms 91 over that person calling their name out in the appropriate place in the scriptures..

Pray the entire chapter of Psalms 91 over their life and pray Psalms 103:1-5 and Acts 16:31.

Pray what comes to your heart and mind. You know what they are dealing with. You know their past. You may know what gave the devil access to rule their lives.

Finish your prayer with,

In the name of Jesus/Yeshua I pray, Amen.

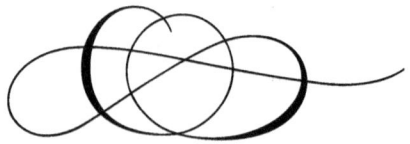

The Spell is Broken

> *Heavenly Father, I thank you for the privilege of coming boldly before Your throne to obtain Mercy & Grace in this time of need. You are King of kings, Lord of lords and a good, good Father!*

Prayer

In the name of Jesus/Yeshua, I command all evil spirits to leave me now. Any witchcraft by food (food or drink given to me which I wasn't aware was witchcraft) be removed from my body now.

Vomit when you feel the urge, don't hold it in. Tell God what symptoms you are experiencing; mental fog, depression, schizophrenia, seeing black shadows, spirits, feeling of someone following you.

Ask God to forgive you and to show you if there is anything you need to throw away (that is giving demons access to you) - pictures, ornaments, gifts, souvenirs, trinkets, statues, furniture, charms, or letters. I don't care how much it cost or who gave it to you, no excuses. Your freedom is worth more than the devil using subtle ways to gain access to your soul to ruin your life or just hinder and frustrate you at every hand.

Listen to God. Anything He tells you, just do it, even if you don't understand why. It is for your own good to obey HIM. He has ONLY your best interest at heart.

~ Continue Praying ~

Cleanse me with the blood of Jesus/Yeshua, (ask HIM to cleanse everything that comes to mind; your mind, eyes, ears, mouth, uterus, vagina/penis, anus, colon, belly, hands, nose, membranes, molecules, every artery, and vein).

Cleanse me with the blood of Jesus/Yeshua and make me whole.

Release Your Warring Angels in the name of Jesus/Yeshua to destroy every demon, principality, and power that comes against me, my family or _____ (name the person).

In the name of Jesus/Yeshua I pray, Amen.

The Spell is Broken

There are persons, places, and things that you need to give up. God is trying to set you free, but you feel addicted and helpless to them. Let the addiction go.

You may feel that you are being held hostage by your investment (whoever/whatever it is that you put your blood, sweat, and tears into).

At the end of the day, God does have an issue with it. That is all that matters. You MUST obey Him. Be encouraged by this thought. What you must give up is nothing in comparison to what HE has for you.

Pray what comes to your mind, whether it's a vision that flashes before your eyes, memories that pop up or dreams you've had. They can all assist you in how to pray. End your prayer with,

"In the name of Jesus/Yeshua I pray, Amen"

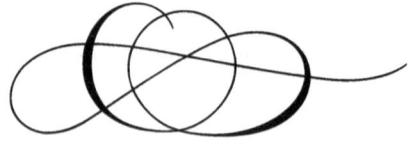

Tug of War

Heavenly Father, I thank you for the privilege of coming boldly before Your throne to obtain Mercy & Grace in this time of need. You are King of kings, Lord of lords and a good, good Father!

~ *Prayer* ~

I come to you in the name of Jesus/Yeshua. God, I don't understand, but I'm willing to obey. I keep feeling You tugging at my heart about _____ (name the person or situation). It seems to me that what I think is good is not the best You have for me. I have grown attached, comfortable, and tied to _____ (fill in the blank with your issue).

Just when I thought I was on track with _____ (name the person or situation) and could exhale, I needed to uproot and make changes again. I'm not good with being flexible, spontaneous, or feeling out of control.

Help me trust You in EVERY aspect of my life. I was created by You and for Your pleasure. I surrender to You.

It's my desire to do Your will and obey YOU. Show me the truth concerning _____ (name where ever you need clarity). Let there be light in every dark place in my heart concerning _____ (name the person or situation). Remove deception, and the lies I tell myself concerning _____ (name the person or situation).

I give you permission to take those things I find hard to release, and remove those things from me that are not pleasing to You. Once you remove them, help me never to chase them and reconnect myself back to the ungodly, temporary pleasure that keeps me trapped and always wanting more.

Put me where I need to be, show me what I need to see. Let me meet who I need to know, show me where I need to go and grow. Reveal to me who I need to let go, and give me the wisdom to know the difference.

In the name of Jesus/Yeshua I pray, Amen.

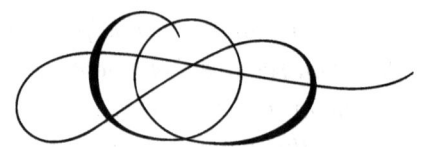

Freedom from Masturbation or Perversion

> *Heavenly Father, I thank you for the privilege of coming boldly before Your throne to obtain Mercy & Grace in this time of need. You are King of kings, Lord of lords and a good, good Father!*

Freedom from Masturbation or Perversion

God/Yahweh downloaded this thought to me: There are God given desires, but what happens when the desires that are God-given are NOT God-driven?

You struggle within trying to figure out minute by minute, day by day who you are going to let drive, aka control, your desires. It's all about control and power. The power is yours, God gave it to you. The question is, who will you give permission to use your power (to choose how you will use your free will), God or the devil?

You want to be in control, yet you feel like a hamster in a wheel going nowhere, repeating cycles of failure. The devil wants to be in control, giving you a TEMPORARY thrill with its pleasures and ultimately it leads you to death, spiritually and sometimes physically (John 10:10, stealing, killing and destroying your God-given destiny and purpose in God). Every day you have death and life before you, and God tells you to choose life. (Deuteronomy 30:19)

It's an open-book (Holy Bible) test.

Sex is God-given, but NOT always God-driven!

Often times we allow, or by force we participate in destructive practices.

We go outside of the boundaries set by God/Yahweh to protect us from the enemy of our soul. When the enemy is allowed to drive our desires, we become defiled.

I come to You in the name of Jesus/Yeshua asking for Your help. I can't do this on my own. I desire to live holy and pure before You without spot or wrinkle. I have gotten so comfortable in this behavior, and I justify it because _____ (name your reason, excuse, rational, or whatever happened to you).

I desire to be free, I can't fight spirits with my fists, knives, guns, and earthly things.

I need Your help God/Yahweh and ask for Your Spirit to destroy the works of these perverted spirits that come against me.

Freedom from Masturbation or Perversion

I need help and ask for Your discipline to get the works of my flesh conquered. Forgive me, God/Yahweh. I have given unclean spirits access and legal right to operate in and through me. I was a willing captive of sexual impurity and its bosom-buddy spirits of fantasy, lust, idolatry, masturbation, adultery, fornication, homo-sexuality, lesbianism, incest and harlotry. In the name of Jesus/Yeshua, I command you spirits of _____ (name above spirits and any that you need to that aren't listed) to leave me now and God/Yahweh, fill me with Your Spirit of Holiness and Purity.

I didn't know that by default, I let these nasty spirits in when I _____ (read/watched pornography, participated in acts of sodomy, allowed someone to perform immoral sexual acts on me). If it was done against your will - I'm sorry that happened to you, please don't blame God.

I confess that I did it, and I was wrong. I admit it is sin and that I am defiled and need to be purged and cleansed from all filth, defilement, and unrighteousness.

In Romans 12:1 NLT, Your word says,

"And so, dear brothers and sisters, I plead with you to give your bodies to God/Yahweh because of all He has done for you. Let them (your bodies) be a living and holy sacrifice – the kind He will find acceptable. This is truly the way to worship Him."

Freedom from Masturbation or Perversion

God, I know we must use spirits to fight spirits. Please release Your Angels. Release Angels of purity and holiness to fight on my behalf (or name the person you are praying for).

Release your warring angels to do battle and destroy the influence of evil spirits and the effects they have had on me in regards to lust, masturbation, sodomy, bestiality, _____ (whatever you struggle with, it can be more than masturbation -- say what you feel led to say).

Lord, release Your warring angels to destroy the spirits that come to defile me and have sex with me in my sleep and dreams. I renounce any covenant I made with them knowingly or unknowingly, in the name of Jesus/Yeshua.

I confess and admit that I enjoy masturbating. I deceived myself into thinking it's okay because it feels good, it relaxes me, it relieves stress, it helps me sleep and _____ (name what it does for you). I command the spirit of deception and rebellion against God's word to stop in Your operation and desist in your maneuver against me.

I desire to please You, God/Yahweh, with my body, thoughts, words, actions, and character, both spiritually and naturally. I want to be a vessel without spot or wrinkle. No longer do I want to do what does not please You.

Lord, please forgive my iniquities, redeem my life from destruction, and make me free. In the name of Jesus/Yeshua I pray, Amen.

Freedom from Masturbation or Perversion

Here are a few practical things to do when you feel tempted:

- Pray immediately and stop preparing to do it.
- Stop having phone sex.
- Don't have perverted things on your mind before you close your eyes.
- Get rid of the items you use; lollipops, pleasure toys, pickles, cucumbers, etc.
- Remove the pillow from between your legs.
- Change your position when you feel the urge coming. Get up out of the bed and Pray.
- Exercise, tire yourself out.
- Do so many push-ups that your arms, hands, and body are too tired to sin.
- Lastly, change your thoughts, stop making excuses in your head to justify it. Agree with God/Yahweh and His perspective on the matter. Make the sin your enemy and stop looking at it as your friend.

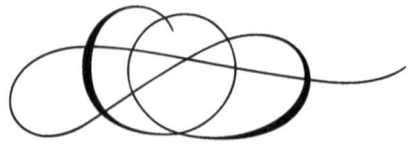

Stop! You're Under Arrest!

> *Heavenly Father, I thank you for the privilege of coming boldly before Your throne to obtain Mercy & Grace in this time of need. You are King of kings, Lord of lords and a good, good Father!*

Stop! You're Under Arrest!

Whether it's someone at home, work, church or a personal encounter on the street, we may have to use this prayer. If you don't need it now, save it and put it in your pocket for later.

Always pray in advance. Pray before a business or church meeting, a phone call, or any situation that you feel may become heated for whatever reason. This prayer works great, especially in personal relationships (marriages, children, in-laws, neighbors, etc.). No one can get on your nerves like your blood relatives. There may be times where things are misunderstood and taken out of context.

X-Rated Prayers

Here's a quick prayer that I say, and it works for me:

∼ *Prayer* ∼

Heavenly Father, I ask that you would be my refuge and my shield. Release Your angels to fight for me. Let me stay in Your peace and not be moved into negative emotions.

Say, you demon spirits of _____ (name whatever the root is or what you sense is the ruling spirit, characteristic the person is known for or the spirit operating at the time; anger, pride, rejection, attention seeking, fear, easily offended, fighting, wrath, etc.)

Stop! You're Under Arrest!

I command you to stop in your operation and desist in your maneuvers against _____ (name the person or situation). We will not partner with your spirits.

We partner with and release righteousness, joy, peace, understanding, Godly wisdom and unity. _____ (name the opposite of the negativity the person is demonstrating or acting out.)

In the name of Jesus/Yeshua I pray, Amen.

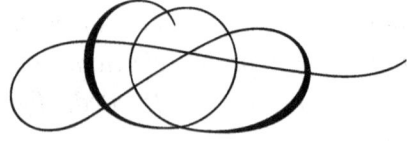

Your Breath Stinks

To Whom Have You Given Authority to Use Your Breath?

> *Heavenly Father, I thank you for the privilege of coming boldly before Your throne to obtain Mercy & Grace in this time of need. You are King of kings, Lord of lords and a good, good Father!*

I admit and confess that I have sinned in my thoughts, words, and actions. The words of my mouth and the meditations of my heart have not been acceptable in Your sight. Your word says,

"Let everything that has breath praise the Lord." (Psalms 150:6 KJV)

I have been using my breath to do the opposite of praise, and my complaining and fear has caused a stench in Your nostrils.

I have allowed fear of _____ (name what you fear) to torment me and take me down a wrong path. God/Yahweh release Your Light in every dark place in my mind, will, and emotions.

You have been showing me the motives and intent of my heart, and I am not setting a good example.

I no longer desire to be this way. I have let any and everything fly out of my mouth with no regard of how it hinders my prayers for myself or others. I have been using my breath to release a stench in the atmosphere, giving the enemy ammunition. I no longer want to use my breath, aka words, to agree with or partner with the devil. I desire to use my words to bring LIFE, not death.

"The tongue can bring death and life, those who love to talk will reap the consequences."
(Proverbs 18:21 NLT)

"Death and life are in the power of the tongue: and they that love it shall eat the fruit thereof."
(Proverbs 18:21 KJV)

The root cause of most anger is fear, and Your word says that You did NOT give me the spirit of fear, but of power, love, and a sound mind.
(2 Timothy 1:7 KJV)

Always remember,

Out of the abundance of the heart, the mouth speaks.
(Matthew 12:34 KJV)

Listen to yourself, you will find out what's in your heart.
(Luke 6:45 KJV)

Help me trust in You Lord with all my heart and lean NOT on my own understanding, but in all my ways acknowledge You, and You will direct my path.
(Proverbs 3:5-6 KJV)

I am so used to being in control and handling everything, and not depending on anyone. (It's PRIDE) I'm sorry. Please forgive me.

I've realized there are some unresolved issues that are deeply suppressed, embedded in my soul, subconscious, and volition that need to be uprooted and healed.

I can't do it on my own. It's hard cutting away the defensive walls and things I have put up so no one would see my Achilles heel. It's hard facing the truth about _____ (fill in the blank regarding your situation). Help me, Lord!

In the name of Jesus/Yeshua I pray, Amen.

Sidebar: This world is governed by words, both written and spoken. The Word of God tells us that the worlds were formed by HIS words.

"By faith, we understand that the entire universe was formed at God's command, that what we now see did not come from anything that can be seen." (Hebrews 11:3 NLT)

What you speak, whether good or evil, creates something in the atmosphere. Words are a vital part of our everyday lives. Words are seeds and they take root in your heart and life, they grow as you water them or die as you uproot them. To counteract and deactivate the negative words (death/darkness) spoken, thought, or even written against you, you must find a scripture in God's Word (Life/Light) that opposes them.

Whether it was you or someone else who spoke them, forgiveness is key. Forgive yourself. Forgive the offender who may have spoken evil over you.

For example, if someone tells you that you will never amount to anything, your response is found within the Scriptures:

"I can do all things through Christ which strengthens me."
(Philippians 4:13 KJV)

It is important to fill yourself with the Word of God. Encourage yourself with words that edify you and build you up.

It is written in God's Word,

"For I know the thoughts that I think towards you, thoughts of peace and not of evil to give you an expected end."
(Jeremiah 29:11 KJV)

Another scripture to speak over yourself is,

"'No weapon that is formed against thee shall prosper, and every tongue that shall rise against thee in judgment thou shalt condemn. This is the heritage of the servants of the Lord, and their righteousness is of Me', sayeth the Lord."
(Isaiah 54:17 KJV)

You can also say,

> *I break the power of every negative word, thought — spoken or written — against me in the name of Jesus/ Yeshua. Lord, release your angels to do battle and destroy the enemy's plots, plans, and schemes against me. Let every word spoken for my destruction be canceled and inoperative now. Let the seed (words are seeds) and root of those words be destroyed and removed from my life. In the name of Jesus/Yeshua I pray, Amen.*

X-Rated Prayers

The more you pray the Word of God, the more it transforms your mind, heart, and spirit. It increases your faith and charges your spiritual battery.

God's Word is spirit and life.

"The Spirit alone gives eternal life. Human efforts accomplish nothing. And the very words I have spoken to you are spirit and life."
(John 6:63 NLT)

Prayer changes you before it changes anything or anyone else.

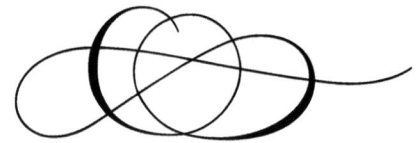

I Thought I Got Away with Murder!

> *Heavenly Father, I thank you for the privilege of coming boldly before Your throne to obtain Mercy & Grace in this time of need. You are King of kings, Lord of lords and a good, good Father!*

Prayer

I come to You with a broken heart, knowing the reason I had an abortion (which is really murder) was because I (fill in the blank with your situation) _____ (I didn't trust You to provide) and I _____ (was selfish). I'm so sorry. I'm overwhelmed with grief, shame, fear, and _____ (regret). I know my excuses will not justify my actions. Although You may understand, I know You don't agree.

God, please forgive me. I was selfish. I was scared, and I did what I thought was best at the time due to _____ (my financial state, career or lack thereof). God, I'm so sorry. I admit I am guilty of murder. I'm a murderer Lord, I'm so sorry. Please forgive me for shedding innocent blood.

I wasn't thinking of it as murder when I made the decision. Wash my conscious, soul, and heart clean with the blood of Jesus/Yeshua from this crime.

Talk to God/Yahweh about your reasoning. Pour out your heart to Him. Was it an inconvenience for you to be pregnant at the time? If so, why?

Was it because you didn't trust God?

Confess whatever the reasoning was to God. Admit your guilt and the part you played in the decision. Was it fear based? Was it because of what a doctor said? I experienced that also – a doctor told me my second first-born's brain was larger on one side than the other, and to abort him. I did not listen to the doctor. I kept my baby, prayed about it and today he is normal, handsome, intelligent, and strong. Thanks be to God.

Was it because you were raped? Say whatever else comes to you, and pray. Pour out your heart and soul before God and stop replaying over and over in your head how old the child would be if you had not aborted him/her. They are in Heaven waiting for you if you make it, and they forgive you. You will see them again and get to raise them. God is amazingly faithful and forgiving. End your prayer with,

"In the name of Jesus/Yeshua I pray, Amen."

Please Allow Me to Testify

I know how you feel – I had two abortions. I'm not boasting, nor am I proud of it. Back then I said, "God, if You forgive me, I won't do that ever again." Then I became pregnant with my first-born son, and I kept him. I call him my promise I made to God. He is a champion. He's more than a conqueror. He is handsome, intelligent, and in a lot of ways, he is the male version of me. I just want to encourage you, once God forgives you, also forgive yourself.

If you or someone you know is pregnant and they are contemplating an abortion, share this testimony with them. I was separated at the time I became pregnant and had financial struggles.

I had settled in my mind that I would have an abortion, because I didn't want the father to think I was trying to trap him. I had called for the appointment and received the T.O.P. (Termination of Pregnancy) confirmation number.

I also didn't want to look foolish by keeping a baby by someone that I wasn't going to be in a relationship with as a family. I couldn't see how I would be able to afford pampers, daycare, food, clothes, etc.

X-Rated Prayers

I prayed and gave God my list of reasons why I would have an abortion. I ran down all the logical explanations, as if it would make HIM agree with me. When I think back, I realize how foolish I was telling the Creator of the universe what I couldn't afford, instead of asking HIM for help. It's like being married to a billionaire and telling him I can't keep his baby because I don't have money. What an Insult. Anyway, He responded, and said to me, "I will forgive you, but the blood will be on your hands for every soul he would have reached for Me."

I was stunned, and instantly I had a resolve in my soul to know somehow that everything would be alright. I never missed a meal, didn't get evicted, and all of our needs and desires have been met until this day. I am so glad I didn't murder my son. He is amazing in every way - smart, handsome, and full of God's wisdom.

Give the baby up for adoption, but don't murder him/her. Some people say, "I can do what I want with MY body," but the truth is, it's NOT YOUR body. The baby has his/her OWN body.

If the baby is a result of rape, either way you will have to recover from the mental anguish. Don't add murder to the list.

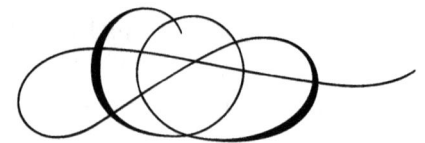

Spiritual Homicide/Suicide "In the Church"

> *Heavenly Father, I thank you for the privilege of coming boldly before Your throne to obtain Mercy & Grace in this time of need. You are King of kings, Lord of lords and a good, good Father!*

Spiritual Homicide/Suicide

"Spiritual Homicide and Suicide IN THE CHURCH" sounds like an oxymoron. In the church, the things that should be killed via homicide or suicide is ALL SIN, Iniquity, Transgressions, SELFishness, Humanism, Idolatry, Pride and EXCUSES for sin. We are to rebuild a more sure foundation in Jesus Christ/Yeshua, and be reconciled unto the True and Living God. We should not be involved in killing (accidental death during friendly-fire) or murdering (intentionally plotting and planning the demise of someone) our own brothers and sisters.

We are called to be a LIVING WILLING SACRIFICE, but as usual, the devil perverts the plan of God using his willing workers to assist him. We thought that by coming to church we escaped the world and its lusts. Instead, we just transferred them into the church and changed the name of the lusts. In some churches, NOT all, money laundering, disguised as tithe and offering, is used to pay to people who "fleece the sheep".

Fornication and adultery are justified as, "God knows my needs and His grace, mercy and forgiveness covers and condones it all!" That's a big fat LIE!!

Lying is disguised as "using wisdom."

Pride and Arrogance are disguised as "anointing and power in/with God." We think we can live like a loose cannon, flowing in God's gift (Holy Spirit) without being defiled. WRONG! Do you really think God/Yahweh condones your life of darkness? He does NOT!

Entitlement and Emotional/Psychological Manipulation are called humility.

Good preaching and articulation WITHOUT the character of Jesus/Yeshua are believed to be accepted and tolerated by God because "we all have issues," so they say. When did it become acceptable to use a microphone and hide behind a clergy collar and robe, while using buzz words like "kingdom assignment" and titles like "Apostles," "Prophets," "Pastors," "Teachers," and "Evangelists"?

Spiritual Homicide/Suicide

The devil is attempting to do an inside job to get the church to destroy itself, but he is a liar. The stage is set, the actors are playing their roles and they will soon be exposed as frauds. It's time out for warlocks, witches, leeches, pimps, spiritual assassins, cannibals and snipers in the pulpit, that are leading people away from the TRUE and LIVING GOD.

In the church, some people will step over those that are wounded and drowning in their own blood, letting them die. If gossip and back-biting had teeth, people would be eaten alive. People kill one another with their words, and get others to partner with them. The devil, operating through a so-called child of god (not Yahweh) will spiritually slit the throat of a person and glory in their death (spiritual homicide). Is that the nature of Jesus/Yeshua? Absolutely NOT. It's the nature of the devil, the one who comes to steal, kill and destroy.

X-Rated Prayers

There are times when the cares of life and the traumatic experiences people encounter may cause them to consider suicide. They don't want to live anymore, they feel hopeless and useless and don't see any way that things will get better. Some cry out to God/Yahweh, and some don't.

There are times when some have pulled the trigger, but it was jammed. Others have taken pills intending to overdose, yet, to their surprise, they woke up the next day. When they have come to an end of themselves that is the place where God can say, "Since you don't want your life anyway, give it to me and allow me to do something GREAT with it." Conversely, the devil is there to cause them to commit suicide. If they won't commit suicide, the enemy of our souls will try to oppress them until they become a dead-man/woman walking (dead to God/Life and alive to the devil/darkness). That's backwards.

Those that decide to give their life to God/Yahweh come into the church looking for restoration. They don't want to be looked at as lower-class church citizens. We need to see them from God/Yahweh's perspective, and draw out of them the gifts they possess. We need to teach them how to use their gifts for righteousness, not unrighteousness.

Spiritual Homicide/Suicide

Many have started out well in God/Yahweh and were turned away by those who falsely represent Him. That is the ultimate trick of the devil; to use God-like things against you. Since the devil couldn't get people to commit suicide before they started going to church, he won't quit. He follows them into the church to get a temporary high, yet they are not fully healed from the root cause of the issues in their life.

When someone has unresolved issues in their life that usually means they hid it, and God/Yahweh wasn't allowed to heal what was suppressed. Manipulative Leaders will listen to members' problems and use what is suppressed against them. This is so sad and heartbreaking. They are now ready to commit spiritual suicide and become hopeless in the pursuit of the True and Living God. All because a so-called representative of God MISrepresented the God of the Universe.

Prayer

Heavenly Father, God of all creation, Master of the Universe, All I want is YOU, NOT man's misinterpretation of you. Lead me to those who are truly your servants that will lead me to life everlasting. Lead me to where You have servants after YOUR heart that will help me make it to heaven, to those who won't use and abuse me for my money, talents or influence.

I have been so drained and at wit's end, burnt out and ready to throw in the towel because of man's way of doing things, yet branding it with Gods/Yahweh's name. I don't know who I can talk to about this. (Pour out your heart to the Father about your detailed scenario, whether it's regarding spiritual homicide or suicide. Don't hold back.)

~ Continue to Pray ~

I need your help, guidance, wisdom and boldness to obey You as You lead me to Freedom in every area of my life.

End your prayer by saying,

In the name of Jesus/Yeshua I pray, Amen.

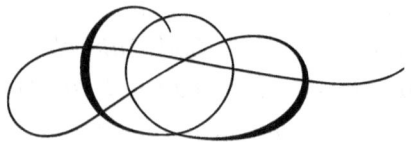

I'm Awake but I Can't Get Up
Demons or Sleep Paralysis

> *Heavenly Father, I thank you for the privilege of coming boldly before Your throne to obtain Mercy & Grace in this time of need. You are King of kings, Lord of lords and a good, good Father!*

Prayer

God, send your Angels to fight for me and render these demons, powers, and principalities tormenting me in my sleep, helpless in the name of Jesus/Yeshua.

God, send Your warring Angels to protect my family and I. Destroy the works of any evil spirits and principalities that plot against us.

Whatever I did to give these evil spirits legal access, reveal it to me so I can stop it, and shut the spiritual doors I opened. I'm sorry Lord for whatever I participated in, read, watched, thought, said, or did. Remove the fear from me of going to sleep. In your Word, You said You give Your beloved sweet sleep and they shall lay down and NOT be afraid. I believe Your Word.

"When thou liest down, thou shall not be afraid; yea, thou shalt lie down, and thy sleep shall be sweet"
Proverbs 3:24 KJV

In the name of Jesus/Yeshua I pray, Amen.

If you are asleep and struggle to wake up:

Keep saying in your mind – Jesus/Yeshua, Help me!

I plead the blood of Jesus/Yeshua, the Messiah against you, evil spirits!

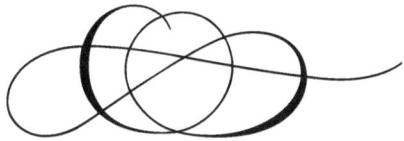

General Declarations to Say Daily

Heavenly Father, I thank you for the privilege of coming boldly before Your throne to obtain Mercy & Grace in this time of need. You are King of kings, Lord of lords and a good, good Father!

While sitting in my car one day, I asked God, "What prayer can I say to You that You want to answer? I'm always saying what I want, but what do You want me to ask for or say to You?" His reply was,

Align me where I need to be to receive what You have for me.

You can also add to that,

Align me to where I need to be, so that others will receive through me what You have for them.

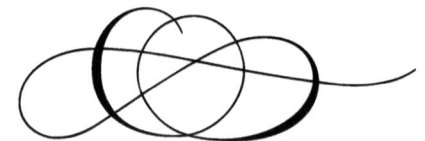

I've Fallen and I Want to Get Up!

> *Heavenly Father, I thank you for the privilege of coming boldly before Your throne to obtain Mercy & Grace in this time of need. You are King of kings, Lord of lords and a good, good Father!*

Prayer

I want to be rid of _____ (name your sin or whatever it is that weighs you down or hinders you). It's wrong. Help me lose the desire and enjoyment for _____ (whatever happened to open the door to this behavior/action, and confess/admit it if you know, or ask God to reveal it).

God, release your Angels of sanctification, purity, integrity, and holiness to destroy the demons of lust, adultery, seduction, porn, lying, hatred, gossip, prejudice, homosexuality, idolatry _____ (fill in the blank with your issue if it's not listed here).

Sever everything in me that gives those demons access to me. Sever every demonic unlawful, distracting spirit (Anything unlawful you do that gives demons lawful access STOP IT NOW - S.I.N.).

Sever all destiny stealing relationships. Cut the cord(s) that connects us, release the fire of God to burn it up.

I veto every demonic legislation written, spoken, or thought against my life (or whomever you are praying for). Cleanse our spirit, soul, and body from hereditary bloodline sin and its activity in me and my children's lives with the Blood of Jesus/Yeshua, which is a weapon of mass destruction.

In the name of Jesus/Yeshua I pray, Amen.

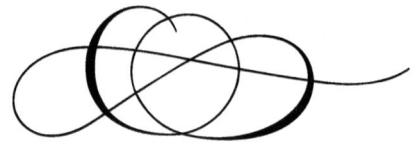

God, it's All Your Fault

> *Heavenly Father, I thank you for the privilege of coming boldly before Your throne to obtain Mercy & Grace in this time of need. You are King of kings, Lord of lords and a good, good Father!*

I know it is appointed unto man to die. We all must go eventually, but I need help dealing with this. I feel like a piece of my heart is missing. It feels like I can't breathe, sometimes. The tears, I know, are a human emotion You gave us as a pressure-release valve and stress reliever, but this hurts so bad.

I miss _____ (name the person and the role they played in your life) like crazy. I just don't understand how to process this pain. I need Your Grace.

I know grief counselors say there are stages of grief: denial, anger, hurt, acceptance, etc. but at the stage I'm in now, I can't see beyond what I'm feeling. Help me, I don't know all the words to express to You, God. I just feel numb, confused, robbed, helpless, useless, and stuck. I can't think straight.

Forgive me if I've made _____ an idol in my life and gave them the place in my life that You should have had – that wasn't my intention. I didn't realize that's what I was doing. (For those who didn't idolize a person can skip that part.)

Get me through this God, I know Your word says that You will never leave me, nor forsake me. I'm holding You to that.

As humans, we like to blame You, God, for everything because we say You can stop things from happening. It's selfish to think that way, because You gave man free will to do things. You didn't create robots that You could control. You gave us the free will to choose our actions and responses.

Note: Pour your heart out before God. He is not intimidated by your emotions or the foul language you may speak in anger. He does not think like a critical, judgmental human being. End your prayer by saying, in the name of Jesus/Yeshua I pray, Amen.

God, It's All Your Fault

Many say you can't or shouldn't question God. I disagree with that statement. Jesus/Yeshua questioned God while on the cross. He said, "WHY has Thou forsaken Me??" That's a question, isn't it? Now, I am not saying you may get an answer that you are looking for, but you can question HIM. I heard a testimony of a woman who was struck with disease and she questioned God and asked Him, "WHY is this happening to me?"

Thankfully, she did question God and didn't just sit there suffering then go on to an early grave. She could have said, "Oh well, this must be God's plan for me." She received a response from God telling her that she was struck with the disease because of the unforgiveness she held onto, which gave satan a landing strip in her heart to put his disease.

She opened the door legally to the devil through her unforgiveness and betrayal, instead of pressing into God for healing and restoration. Her questioning God helped her receive the answer. She confessed her sins, and is now healed from the incurable disease and doing well.

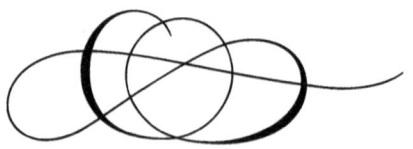

Sleeping With the Enemy

> *Heavenly Father, I thank you for the privilege of coming boldly before Your throne to obtain Mercy & Grace in this time of need. You are King of kings, Lord of lords and a good, good Father!*

Sleeping with the Enemy

You need to guard and protect the gates (eyes, ears, mouth, body and sexual organs) to your soul. Do not fill it with filth, violence and sexual impurity from video games, books, movies and television shows full of violence, sex and witchcraft. People let ungodly things play while they sleep, which contaminates their unconscious minds and they don't realize it or either they don't care.

You MUST counteract it by putting what's clean in your soul the same way you put in evil – by reading the Word of God (The Holy Bible) by worshipping our Heavenly Father with your life and by listening to worship music. You must also be mindful only to watch what brings edification to your soul.

God, I confess, and admit I am guilty of being careless by letting any and everything come into my spirit, soul, body, conscious and subconscious through books I've read, conversations I've listened to and/or participated in, TV shows and movies I've watched, video games I've played, and allowed my children to do the same.

I figured it was okay because it was the norm. We are inundated with filth from the prince of the power of the air (the devil), which is his plan being manifested and we walk right into the trap.

Give me the discipline to turn off the evil influences and guard my soul. Give me the desire to participate with what pleases you, God. Help me to read Your word and obey it.

Sleeping with the Enemy

Wash me with the water of Your Word as I read it. Change my spirit, soul, appetite, and cravings from unholy to Holy.

Help me to listen to music that tells me who You are and who I am in You. (Search YouTube for Kimberly and Alberto Rivera, Grace Williams, Jason Upton, Paul Wilbur and others under soaking music.)

Forgive me for defiling myself, offending Your spirit, and not realizing my body is Your temple. Your Spirit dwells in me and I have been subjecting You to all types of defilement.

Initially, I felt uneasy, but I ignored it, not realizing it was Your Spirit telling me not to do it or watch things that my lust enjoyed.

The more I ignored your prompts, the more I became dull in my conscious towards You, and I became desensitized until I deceived myself into believing there's nothing wrong with it.

God, please release Your Angels to surround me and protect me from any evil spirit that seeks to defile me. I no longer want to be a vessel for evil to live in. I no longer want to be a container for evil. I desire to commit to You, God. I break covenant with and renounce the works of darkness and evil that I partnered with and I ask You to forgive me. God, I'm sorry, I was wrong.

I took pleasure in it (name whatever your "it" is), and I preferred it over pleasing and obeying You.

Sleeping with the Enemy

Make me whole in my spirit, soul, body, mind, conscious and volition that I may be one with You in my thoughts, words, and actions. Let everything I entertain please you. I no longer desire to find pleasure in darkness.

Set a guard in my heart that won't allow me to stay and be content in darkness. Protect me as I sleep and let my dreams be those of You speaking to me and not of the evil and filth I filled myself with.

In the name of Jesus/Yeshua I pray, Amen.

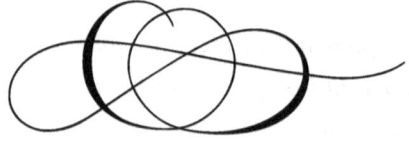

Pillow Talk

Tears Are Liquid Prayers

Heavenly Father, I thank you for the privilege of coming boldly before Your throne to obtain Mercy & Grace in this time of need. You are King of kings, Lord of lords and a good, good Father!

Pillow Talk

Don't allow divorce (name your situation: separated, widowed, etc.) to cause you to feel as though you are damaged goods. Whether the divorce was bitter or smooth, whether you initiated it or were served the papers to your surprise, don't start having trust issues and looking at others sideways. Allow yourself to heal and be by yourself. Don't go jump into someone else's bed because you can't take being alone.

I understand how it feels – you are afraid to be alone and desire to jump at this person giving you attention because you don't know how long it will be before you get another chance at love. Many things are rolling around in your head; most likely fear based. We are of a certain age now and no one has time to be someone's girlfriend or boyfriend.

When you have been married or in a monogamous relationship (name your scenario: shacking-up, common-law marriage, domestic partner, etc.) for any length of time, and you are used to a certain intimacy and companionship, it's hard to be by yourself. You feel vulnerable and afraid. Sometimes out of desperation, you use the wrong things to fill that void.

~ Prayer ~

I am of a certain age and I desire to be married (or name your situation). I haven't been on the dating scene for a while, so I feel like a fish out of water. The game (so to speak) has new rules and I don't know how to play. I don't want to have to go through 10-to-20 people to get to the right person. It's emotionally draining, and there are so many snakes in the grass out there. I love easily and hard and I catch feelings quickly. I don't know how to be in date mode. I'm all in or out; I'm on or I'm off. I can't take being in date mode for more than five years. I'm used to being married and in a consistent, secure covenant.

Pillow Talk

God, I don't know how to act like just a girlfriend (if you are a female praying) or boyfriend (if you are a male praying) while dating, because I have been married so long (or name your scenario). I come across as needy and easy to meet another's needs, and that opens the door to be taken advantage of.

Lord, please protect me from the selfish (Idolatrous) desires I have, and from being manipulated by people while I go through the healing process. I want attention, affection and companionship. One touch the right way, I know I will be in somebody's bed with my legs up, wrapped around their neck (women praying) or I will be running up in something, blowing somebody's back out (men praying).

HELP ME!!! (I have used these two words as the shortest, most powerful prayer I've ever prayed.) Heal me, make me whole, mind, soul, and spirit. Whoever my future husband or wife is, bring them to me when I start dating so we can date to marry. I don't want to waste time interviewing various prospects. Since tears are liquid prayers, Lord, let them speak for me. If pillows could talk, You would hear my heart, the things I can't think to say.

Strengthen me where I am weak, protect me out here in these streets, remove me from Satan's seat, cleanse my mind from defeat.

In the name of Jesus/Yeshua I pray, Amen.

Pillow Talk

Note: We are seated with Jesus/Yeshua in Heavenly places. Be seated with Him, rest in Him and trust the process. Learn about yourself through the process. Watch your immature, unbelieving reactions and deal with them. When you go through trials and difficulties, you learn about yourself – the good, the bad, and the ugly.

God may be testing your heart, motives, and intents to indicate if your loyalty belongs to Him, yourself, or the devil (enemy of your soul). If your motives are pure from God's standard, fine. If they are not pure motives, fix it. Don't beat yourself up. Be anxious for nothing. Keep praying, believing and expecting to receive grace for discipline, control, and integrity, and not fearing or worrying about how long you will be alone. Get to know yourself and work on your wounds with God's/Yahweh's help.

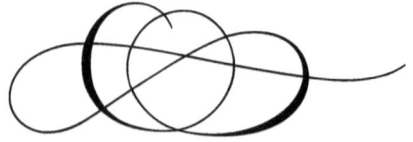

Stop Lying on God

Using Your Position of Authority to Control/Manipulate Others

> *Heavenly Father, I thank you for the privilege of coming boldly before Your throne to obtain Mercy & Grace in this time of need. You are King of kings, Lord of lords and a good, good Father!*

Hebrews 13:17 NLT says,

"Obey your spiritual leaders and do what they say. Their work is to watch over your souls, and they are accountable to God. Give them a reason to do this with joy and not with sorrow. That would certainly not be to your benefit."

Prayer

God/Yahweh, I do all I was taught by Pastors. I give tithe and offerings faithfully. I never miss a service. I do everything they ask me to do. I need help, I know in times past I have been rebellious and hard-headed towards authority, most of all towards You. I didn't always recognize Your voice, Father, when You spoke to me. Please forgive me for ignoring You.

I dismissed Your voice because I wasn't sure if the voice was my own thoughts, the devil, or You. I appreciate You patiently continuing to talk to me until I recognized Your voice more confidently. Now, I have grown accustomed to Your voice, promptings, and impressions.

Stop Lying on God!

Lately, I have been a little confused because when I hear You speak, and attempt to obey Your voice, the church leader causes me to doubt what I hear YOU say. Should I refrain from going to them for advice? I'm beginning to realize, just because some have the title of "Pastor" does not mean they KNOW You intimately. They know OF You, but don't know You intimately. Some are hirelings.

I noticed if they don't have their own deep hunger and thirst for You, they can't relate to me trying to get into a more intimate relationship with You. They are caught up in the administration of church business and the Image of being a Pastor, but they don't have a heart after God.

They used the scripture, Hebrews 13:17 to curtail me and make me feel rebellious if I don't listen.

In my heart, I am truly not trying to be rebellious. I believe the leader wants to control me and keep me from leaving them. I am loyal and it's a struggle trying to figure out what to do. I want to obey you, Lord, yet the leader says if I obey them, then it is the same as obeying God since they are the servants of God. They also said, 'if God has something to tell me, You will tell it to them to relay to me.' I can't be with the Pastor 24/7, and I know YOU talk to ME without them.

That sounds like control and manipulation, aka charismatic witchcraft.

When I tell them it's manipulation, they call me a devil and spread that perspective of me around to others so they will also view me as a devil. I no longer want to be manipulated by them.

Stop Lying on God!

Lord, it hurts to know I am being lied to and misunderstood. To top it off, the leaders used their influence to turn church members, friends, and my own family against me. In order to prove their loyalty to the leadership, they are told to disassociate themselves from others. Help me not become bitter. Lord, be my shield against the arrows of darkness that come against me.

I never expected to get this type of treatment from the church leaders. I only want to know, hear and obey Your voice and build a personal relationship with YOU on my own.

When we have special gatherings, the leader has given false prophesies/predictions concerning our lives, claiming to be words from God. In reality, it is only to keep us under their control.

I feel such an uneasy, dirty feeling in my soul. I know this is NOT a characteristic of God's Spirit, nor is this behavior Gods' heart for us.

Conversely, there can be a service where we have a guest speaker who will give a word from God that is confirmed in my spirit, and the next week, the manipulative minister will rip down everything that was spoken the week before.

When I have addressed how I feel, it doesn't go well, so I remain quiet. Then the leader will say during his message, 'if you leave the church, you will be cursed' (fear-tactic).

God reveal Yourself. Give me Your wisdom and direction in this matter.

Give me boldness to obey You. Let the blinders of manipulation, control, and witchcraft be removed from the heart and mind of the leader. Lead me by Your Spirit to a true Bible-teaching church that's led by YOU.

I want to make it to Heaven. I want to be taught my purpose on this earth. I don't want to waste time, energy and finances being in the wrong place.

In the name of Jesus/Yeshua I pray, Amen.

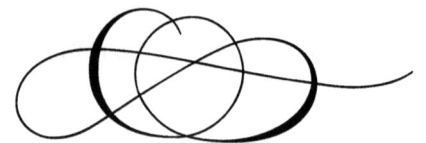

Pick on Someone Your Own Size

**I Will Not Be Bullied
Neither Will I Commit Suicide**

Heavenly Father, I thank you for the privilege of coming boldly before Your throne to obtain Mercy & Grace in this time of need. You are King of kings, Lord of lords and a good, good Father!

Pick on Someone Your Own Size

Are you being bullied?

Know someone who is being bullied?

Are you the bully?

Find scriptures from The Holy Bible that address protection and pray them out loud. When you do so, it releases Angels.

Psalms 103:20 KJV reads,

Bless the Lord, ye His Angels, that excel in strength, that do His commandments, hearkening unto the voice of His word.

How do you give voice to the Word of God/Yahweh? By using your voice to speak the Word of God out loud. When you speak the Word of God, Angels hear it and make it happen. You can't pick up the Bible and wave it in the air and expect it to be heard. You need to say the Scriptures out loud.

Isaiah 54:17 NLT reads,

No weapon turned against you shall succeed.

2 Thessalonians 3:3 NLT reads,

But the Lord is faithful, and he will strengthen you and guard you from the evil one.

Pick on Someone Your Own Size

Deuteronomy 31:6 NLT reads,

So be strong and courageous! Do not panic before them. For the Lord your God will personally go ahead of you. He will neither fail you nor abandon you.

Psalms 59:1 NLT reads,

Rescue me from my enemies, O God: Protect me from those who have come to destroy me.

Psalms 138:7 NLT reads,

Though I am surrounded by troubles, you will protect me from the anger of my enemies. You reach out your hand, and the power of your right-hand saves me.

Psalms 140:4 NLT reads,

O Lord, keep me out of the hands of the wicked. Protect me from those who are violent, for they are plotting against me.

Psalms 91 NLT is a Psalm of Protection. Pray all the scriptures from Psalms 91 over your life if you are being bullied, or if you are praying for someone you know being bullied. Even if you are the bully, pray these scriptures so you don't die or get killed in your sin and go to hell while you are under the control of evil spirits. Don't be a fool for the devil, it's NOT worth it. Stop being a coward for the devil and be courageous for God/Yahweh.

If you encounter someone being bullied, let them know not to be ruled by fear. Let them know that it's the devil operating through a person that bullies others. The person bullying others is really a coward, and hopes to use fear to control others. Let them know not to be manipulated by the threats from bullies, and to tell the authorities immediately.

The bully may say, "Don't tell anyone or I will kill you and your family." Don't get into isolation. Isolation is a trick of the devil to keep you in fear, so he can put more thoughts in your mind to torment you with no one there to help you counteract the negative thoughts. Stay connected to those who walk with the Living God, they will help you dispel darkness and the bully will lose his/her power over your mind.

Pick on Someone Your Own Size

Always, and I mean always, drag darkness into the light and expose its works. Don't internalize stuff and be isolated, because that gives the devil, and the person the devil is using, more power. Light dispels darkness; therefore, even at the cost of being embarrassed or looking like a punk, tell someone who can help you, and if they brush you off and downplay your plea, keep praying Psalms 91. Then ask God to send Warrior Angels and human intervention to help.

No matter what, DO NOT COMMIT SUICIDE, DO NOT GIVE UP ON YOUR LIFE. DO NOT AGREE WITH THE VOICE OF THE DEVIL. The Word of God is a literal weapon that is used by speaking, praying and believing THE WORD.

Note: The principle, concept and application of this prayer can also be applied to mental and physical abuse in a relationship.

His word is spirit and life and will give you life if you believe.
(John 6:63 NLT)

Prayer

If you are being bullied or praying for someone being bullied, address the prayer accordingly (for you or others):

> *You demons of bullying, cowardice, death, embarrassment, envy, fear, hopelessness, insecurity, intimidation, lies, manipulation, murder, suicide and torment, I command you to stop in your operations and desist in your maneuvers (against me or the person you are praying for) in the name of Jesus/Yeshua.*
>
> *Heavenly Father, be my/their shield and refuge. God/Yahweh release your Warring Angels to fight for me and protect me from all evil. I thank you that no weapon formed against me (or the person you are praying for) will prosper.*

Give me (or name the person you are praying for) power, love, and a sound mind, and cast out the spirit of fear from me (or the person you are praying for).

Let them not be afraid to tell others what is going on and to seek help. If family is dismissive and uninterested, please give me someone who I can trust to take this seriously. Heal me (or the person you are praying for) from the hurt and rejection this may cause. In the mighty name of Jesus/Yeshua I pray. Amen.

If you are the bully, pray:

God/Yahweh, I have sinned, and I admit I am wrong. I need your forgiveness for hurting and bullying people. I no longer want to partner with, nor agree with those spirits of intimidation, fear, control, jealousy and murder ruling me and trying to make me a fool for the devil.

Pick on Someone Your Own Size

I will not cut off my life, nor the lives of others and I will not rob myself or others of fulfilling my/their destiny in God/Yahweh. Lord, release your Warring Angels to fight for me and protect me from all evil. Forgive me for allowing the devil to use me to do his work. I no longer want to be a fool for the devil.

Heal me from all hurt, rejection, identity crisis and insecurities within that cause me to treat people with such hate. Remove all demonic blinders off my mind and heart and fill me with your Love. Save me, God/Yahweh. I will no longer hurt, kill or cause others to become bullies.

In the name of Jesus/Yeshua I pray, Amen

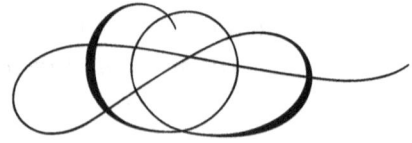

Epilogue

When we come into this world, we are born in sin and shaped in iniquity by default. Sin is our slave master, with satan and the works of our flesh in control of our lives behind the scenes, yet we think we are controlling our own lives.

Many do whatever the enemy of our souls aka, The devil, says or suggests. Some live by the motto: "eat, drink, and be merry" without considering the origin of the motive and intent of our actions.

We think if it feels good, it must be good. That's a lie!! We use the excuse, YOLO (You Only Live Once) to soothe our conscious and justify sin and disobedience against God and our own soul.

We have no clue that we are slaves and prisoners to sin, with no power to break free. The devil is our pimp and we are his prostitute.

Once we realize we are trapped, gagged, tied-up, and entangled in what we thought was pleasure, we then begin our journey to be free from sin's deadly grip. We use our own willpower, and though it may work for a while, it won't bring about a permanent change. It will only mask, disguise, hide itself or suppress the bondage.

Epilogue

At that point, we usually cry out to God for help, if we aren't drowned in pride and we desire true freedom from the inside out.

We recognize our need to forsake (to renounce or turn away from entirely) our sinful, idolatrous and selfish ways (which lead to death), and follow holiness and obedience to God's Holy Word (which leads to Eternal Life). Jesus/Yeshua IS THE WORD OF GOD. We realize our need for Him to purify our hearts and cut off the darkness, death, and sin and fill that space with Himself (His Spirit, Nature, Character, Holiness, Light, Life, Obedience, Purity and Truth).

You can receive the living God into your heart, soul, and life and not only receive what HE can do FOR you, but you can allow HIM to LIVE THROUGH you by being one in/with HIM.

For those of you that are already redeemed (sons of God) and have left the light to keep going back into darkness and agreeing with its lusts and believing the lies of the old creature (your old mindset) ruled by the devil – stop it! Stop opposing the nature of God within you. The devil Is no longer your puppet master once you are redeemed. If you obey the devil, it was your decision to give place to his devices.

For those who have not yielded their lives to God/Yahweh by being reconciled to Him through Jesus/Yeshua, you can do so right now, by an act of your will. You can make a conscious decision to give up your rights to your life and yield control to God/Yahweh, the creator of the Heavens and the earth.

Prayer of Salvation

For everyone who calls on the name of the Lord will be saved.
Romans 10:13 NLT

Nowhere in The Holy Bible is there a prayer labeled, "prayer of salvation". Below I will give a general prayer you can use, feel free to customize it. I think in pictures, so what comes to mind is the story in the Holy Bible, when Peter walked on water. He began to sink when he took his focus off of Jesus/Yeshua and focused on the depth of the water, darkness, and his own inadequacies.

He yelled out/called His name, "Jesus/Yeshua, Help Me! Save me!" He believed in Jesus/Yeshua's ability to save him and wasn't too prideful to call out to HIM for help. He didn't try to handle it on his own and drown.

Prayer of Salvation

Whether you are sinking due to the cares of life, or are on top of the world and feel like you don't need a Savior, we all do. For those who think they can't come to God because they only call on God/Yahweh when they are in trouble, it's totally fine to do so. HE does not think like humans. He wants you to run TO HIM, not away from Him In the times of trouble. Especially when things are going great, stay In HIS face at all times. Let nothing draw you away, not poverty, riches, disappointments, false teachers, world systems – NOTHING!!!

X-Rated Prayers

My ***Prayer of Salvation*** is simply:

God/Yahweh, I want to return home to your Kingdom, where I was before I came to this Earth. You provided a way through your Son, Jesus/Yeshua.

Jesus/Yeshua, save me! Help me and rescue me from myself and from the destruction of my own soul. Break the power of sin and death off my life. Set me free from _____ (name what comes to mind) now and forever. Remove the root and the seed of the bondages and strongholds in my life.

God/Yahweh The Father, Jesus/Yeshua The Son and The Holy Spirit come into my heart and live. Take up residence. Move out everything that is not like you. Fill me with Your light and drive out all darkness and its evil influences. Show me what You created me to do and help me accomplish it.

Prayer of Salvation

I give You my life to live through and help me do what you created me to do. I give you my dreams and aspirations, and I ask that you give me your dreams and desires for my life.

I have done things my way and messed so many thing up. Please get me out of the web I have gotten myself stuck in. Show me what my purpose is on this Earth. What specific part do I play in THIS life?

I want to be a citizen of The Kingdom of Heaven. When I die from this life, I want to come to live with you. Show me how to make it back home to you, Father. I give you my life as a living sacrifice. Make me holy and acceptable in your sight.

I know being a citizen of Heaven, and renouncing my allegiance to the kingdom of darkness and the world with its lusts of the flesh, the lusts of the eyes and the pride of life, will cost me everything. I am willing to give it all up for you, to join the Kingdom of Heaven. Teach me how to be a citizen of your Kingdom and learn your culture. In the name of Jesus/Yeshua I pray. Amen.

Now ask God/Yahweh to lead you to a place that is truly making disciples for HIM and not for themselves.

Seek HIM for a true Bible teaching house church, fellowship, or congregation that is a House of Prayer that allows God/Yahweh to rule and govern all the affairs – one that is not ruled by fear and manipulation (charismatic witchcraft), where the Holy Spirit is welcome to come with his refining fire, pruning knife and rivers of living water. Where you can grow and flourish in the nature, character, and authority of God/Yahweh.

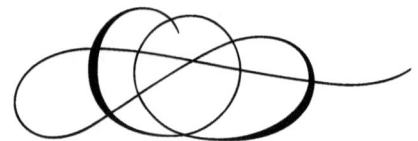

About the Author

Born a native to Essex County, New Jersey, Theresa Billingsley graduated from the Newark Public School System and later from the Bethesda Bible College under the leadership of the late Dr. Nathaniel Screven. It was here where she obtained her Bachelor of Arts in Biblical Theology.

About the Author

Her energetic and outgoing personality afforded her the opportunity to meet many people. It is through those encounters that guided her to discover her call to intercession.

It is the desire of her heart to help others recognize that within them already lies the power to choose freedom and obtain the confidence needed to approach their Heavenly Father.

Theresa believes that every person should approach the Father as a child would, not perceiving Him as a Judge preparing to throw the book at them and sentence them to death. It is through this passion that inspired her first publication, ***X-Rated Prayers***.

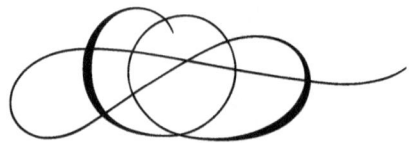